D0793873

A Dash
Through Leaves

FOR ADRIAN
and the accumulation of happiness

A Dash
Through Leaves

By PENNY GRIFFIN

SA PL

PERSEPHONE PRESS
Whispering Pines, NC

I want to thank the women who supported me in this project and for the ways they contributed to my knowledge of Japan, the Japanese Language, haiku poetry, and Buddhism: Dr. Jan Bardsley, Lorraine Harr, Kikuko Imamura, Jackie Matossian, Rebecca Rust, Dr. Janet Zehr, and special thanks to Mary Belle Campbell, Editor-Publisher of Persephone Press.

Some of these Zen-Japanese-style haiku poems have been previously published in the following haiku journals: *Dragonfly: A Quarterly of Haiku; Frog Pond; Ko.*

Calligraphy and Ink Paintings by Mona Wu
Book Design by Tom Tolnay

A Mary Belle Campbell Limited Edition
Published by PERSEPHONE PRESS
53 Pine Lake Drive
Whispering Pines, NC 28327-9388
Tel: 910-949-3993

Available from independent bookstores.

FORWARD

At a time when no easy definitions of haiku exist among writers of haiku in English, there is no awkward space between the classical and the contemporary in Penny Griffin's work. Her haiku remain faithful to basic classical elements as we in the West understand them, yet she proceeds with courage when her purpose calls for original structure.

Penny Griffin believes in the oneness of past, present, and future, and as she says, "the aesthetic integrated into every day life." A student of the Japanese language, she spent time living in a Shinto Temple near Kyoto where she studied the Tea Ceremony, Noh Dance, and calligraphy. She later spent a summer teaching American Art History at Machida's Obirin University in greater Tokyo. A recent retreat at the Namgyal Monastery in Ithaca, New York, strengthened her interest in the Buddhist philosophy and its relation to haiku.

Her work is new with fresh insight yet old with character. Once someone, mistaking haiku for kudzu, asked me if haiku were hard to grow. I would say that it is, and Penny Griffin grows it very well.

Rebecca Rust, Founder
The North Carolina Haiku Society

PREFACE

The Poems

Haiku is not comparable to any Western poetry model. The form is as spontaneous as the flowing brush stroke in a Chinese painting. Borrowed from the Japanese, English haiku is brief, usually divided into three lines with something close to a 5/7/5 syllable count.

In haiku the images are real and concrete; there is no fantasy. Subjects are banal; events are those of everyday life, intimate and immediate. In the best haiku, the poet uses the plain language of the poem to see the ordinary as extraordinary. In the middle of one's daily routine there is transformation to an awareness of life. Every moment offers possibility.

Customarily a season word expands the dimensions of the poem: a woolen coat sets the scene for winter; a water sprinkler recalls the unforgiving heat of summer. The real or implied presence of nature is a reminder of the impermanence of things, the passing of time, and the inevitability of death. Life is as fragile and mutable as a single white cloud passing through the clear blue sky.

The haiku in this collection conform to standard guidelines with some exceptions. Where rules are broken the poet accepts responsibility for making those artistic and personal decisions.

In Chinese and Japanese art there is a long history of uniting poetry, painting and calligraphy. This volume of haiku continues to explore that tradition.

The Calligraphy and Ink Paintings

The poems in this book are divided by sections representing the four seasons and the New Year. The calligraphic figures introducing each section are names of moons that mark seasonal changes according to an ancient Chinese lunar calendar. This calendar was an early attempt by primitive man to understand "the interdependence of earth and sky and the connection between the spiritual, the animate, and the inanimate worlds."[1]

The paintings in this book are done in a traditional Chinese style. The aesthetic principle of Oriental painting is beautifully described by the 1968 Nobel Laureate, Yasunari Kawabata:

> The heart of ink painting is in the space,
> abbreviation, what is left undrawn. In the
> words of the Chinese painter Chin Nung:
> "You paint the branch well and you hear
> the sound of the wind."[2]

My thanks to Mona Wu for capturing the spirit of haiku in her paintings.

Penny Griffin
Winston Salem, N.C.
April 30, 1995

1. Juliet Bredon and Igor Mitrophanow, *The Moon Year* (Shanghai: Kelly and Walsh, 1927) 4.
2. Yasunari Kawabata, *Japan the Beautiful and Myself* (Tokyo, New York & San Francisco: Kodansha International, 1969) 54.

SPRING
Budding Moon

Early spring
green spreads
from tree to tree

Stone for a seat
deep in woods surrounded
by young green ferns

Spring at last
wind chimes
all day long

The white peony
I come away with
dew on my nose

On the kitchen table
a bouquet of peonies
and one busy ant

A broken stem and
still it struggles to open
the peony bud

Bumble bee landing
apple blossom shudders
under the weight

After the rain
cunning scent of honeysuckle
hides in the mist

Long rainy days
purple wisteria gradually
fades to white

Yoshino cherry
in the shade of a great oak
only a few white blossoms

The mirror reflecting
a new spring moon
I lie here sleepless

Commuter's routine
by the roadside wild violets
bloom and fade

Empty vase
pale pink petals scattered
on the compost heap

Spring rain
an old man on the bridge
two lovers below

Fields not yet green
old tobacco barns remain
year after year

I-40 rush hour
pink balloon floats in the median
no strings attached

Spring cleaning
these old blue jeans
I wore in Kyoto

Afternoon nap,
one eye opens on
a red geranium

SUMMER
Dragon Moon

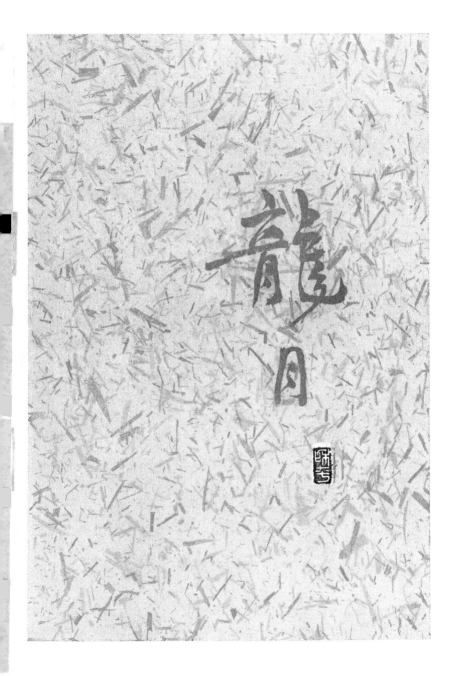

A cloudless summer sky
going back inside
to regain significance

Coolness settles
in spikes of lavender
three feet tall

English village
scented damask roses
grow into trees

Fireflies also
fail to appear
a moonless night

Eclipsed by
firefly maneuvers
a pale new moon

Old empty suitcase
the scent of salt sea water
still clings

Dried rose petals
in the linen drawer
last year's summer

Childhood
memories of rose petals
mother's deep red lips

Just before
petals drop
the heaviness of roses

Linen dress
printed flower pattern
wilts in the heat

Tea in the garden
the metamorphoses
of one white cloud

Fourth of July
stars on the flag rearranged
by a sudden breeze

Summer afternoon
lemon rind shrivels
in the empty glass

Midsummer heat
in the center of the hibiscus
another center

The end of summer
a few bits of dirt
in the spider's web

Last days of summer
a new Freshman Class
we look at one another

Homesick
students prefer to complain
about the heat

Daibutsu of Kamakura [1]
gazes over the ocean
always the ocean

Sightseer in the rain
Buddha's gaze reveals
nothing

1. The "Daibutsu" (great) bronze Buddha at Hase, Kamakura, is a thirteenth century sculpture, 34.6 feet in height. Once enclosed in a wooden hall destroyed shortly after its construction by a tidal wave, this imposing figure has survived natural disasters and exposure to the elements for over 500 years. Today it looms above the tree tops with powerful and calm presence.

Surrounding the Buddha
scent of pine broth
after the rain

After the rain
my face reflected
in the ancient bronze

Buddha rests
on the stone lotus
his countless teachings

Lines of open umbrellas
the hydrangea blossoms
of Meigetsu-in Temple

Last view of Kamakura
all the twilight gathered
into the sea

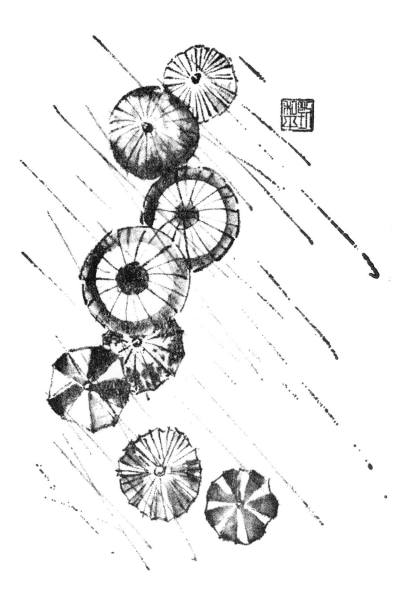

AUTUMN
Harvest Moon

Scattered autumn leaves
assorted colors in a bag
of M & M's

Outside the bakery
everyone passing by
sniffs the autumn air

Off the path
a dash through leaves
just to hear the sound

Scattered over a grave
no traditional arrangements
only petals

Pressed flowers
somebody's memory
crumbles in my hand

Tobacco farmer
stained brown fingers
test the leaf

Indian Summer
dust from the road settles
on chrysanthemums

Just enough wind
to twist a single
red maple leaf

Her bright colored quilts
draped across the porch rail
rustle of autumn leaves

Autumn deepens
along the mountain ridge
lights go out one by one

Overcast sky
mountain cabin's smoke column
mingles with first snow

First snowfall
a forgotten tea kettle
boils dry

Grandpa sleeps in his chair
across the mountain tops
clouds come and go

Orange striped cat
curls around
a point of moonlight

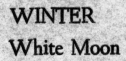

WINTER
White Moon

In drain pipes
water begins to freeze
full winter moon

Late night snack
the smell of oranges
under my fingernails

First snowflakes melt
against the window pane
tea water boils

Winter solstice
a little warmth radiates
from the bedside lamp

Do you mind
a little warmth borrowed
from your side of the bed

Past her bedtime
full moon and three gold stars
on the child's homework

Morning coffee
aroma increases desire
drop by drop

Dial tone
a faint smell of after-shave
remains on the line

Temperature falling
smell of coldness
in the dog's fur

Pine tree's twisted roots
before my grandparents
were born

Winter drizzle
empty soup cans pile up
in the garbage pail

January sun
mounds of dirty snow
melt at the edges

Early morning meditation
my warm breath strikes
cold reality

February drizzle
I stare at the closet where
summer clothes hang

Avoiding people
a sprig of blue cedar
feels cool in her hand

Late winter storm
freezing rain lacquers
japonica blossoms

Death
a snowflake brushes
the palm of my hand

NEW YEAR
Bitter Moon

Traveler
develops non-attachment
only one carry on

No moonlight
a traveler must continue
his journey

Airplane engine
drones the same mantra
for each passenger

Night sky
over the Atlantic
I am part of it

Descent through clouds
the runway glistens black
with rain

Busy Paris Metro
laughing American students
my responsibility

Chilly morning
vendors sell coffee and violets
through train windows

Hotel in Rome
still not recovered
listening to rain

Vatican City
in the holy enclave
children work the crowd

British Museum
smell of roast chestnuts
stops you at the gate

Years end
looking out the window
going back to bed

Times Square
after celebrations
old movies on T.V.

Early morning chill
pages of the diary
clean and white

New wall calendar
its pages contain
my only ocean view

New Years Day
the world remains
as usual

Buddhist priest
during the holidays
his unchanging routine

The haiku within
A DASH THROUGH LEAVES
were typeset by hand in metal
14 pt. Deepdene, a font designed
by Frederic Goudy. Text was printed
letterpress on a V-45 Miehle Vertical
with 80 lb. Mohawk Vellum. Cover stock
is 80 lb. Artemis in radiant white.
Artwork was printed from halftone
engravings in hand-mixed Marvel ink.
Titles & details were printed
on a Chandler & Price in
colors of the season.
Typesetting & printing
by Birch Brook Press,
Delhi, NY.

THE ARTIST

A native of China, Mona Wu came to the United States in 1971. She studied Chinese painting and calligraphy in Hong Kong and has been teaching Chinese painting at the Sawtooth Center for Visual Art in Winston Salem, North Carolina since 1982. Mona is now enrolled at Salem College majoring in Art History.

THE POET

Penny Griffin is an Assistant Professor of Art History at Salem College in Winston Salem, North Carolina, and lives with her husband in Mount Airy, North Carolina. Her poetry has been published in several magazines in the United States and Japan. She is currently editor of "Pine Needles", the newsletter of the North Carolina Haiku Society. A DASH THROUGH LEAVES is her first book of poetry.